Table

MW01592764

About author

Helena was a very good-natured child. She loved nature and animals. People felt better in her presence. Everyone adored that little girl who dreamed of becoming a teacher. When Helena was 8 years old, a terrible accident happened to her. She and her parents went to the country. There was a river nearby and they decided to go boating. When they reached the middle of the river, Helena saw a shoal of fish and leaned over to catch some of them. But suddenly she lost her balance and fell into the water. It was springtime, and the water was too cold and she had a cramp in her left foot. The girl couldn't swim and she started drowning. The last thing she remembers is that she started losing consciousness.

Her parents noticed their daughter's disappearance only a few minutes later since they were immersed in conversation. Helena's father plunged into the water to save her. He pulled her out of the water only 5 minutes later. The girl was breathless and unconscious. Her parents tried to resuscitate her. A few minutes later, her father felt the weak pulse, but the girl was still unconscious. The parents rushed Helena to a local hospital.

The doctors told them that the girl had slipped into a coma and that she could remain in a persistent vegetative state since her brain was damaged due to the lack of oxygen when she was under the water.

Her parents were in deep despair. A week later, when her mother was sitting beside her daughter in the hospital, she fell asleep and saw a dream, in which Susan told her that she would come back soon. Her mother woke up full of hope because she believed in the power of her dreams. Next day, Helena emerged from the coma. Moreover, she was quite well.

After that accident, she became more sensitive. She started perceiving emotions and thoughts of other people. She started seeing prophetic dreams. She knew what her mother would ask her before she even started speaking. Since then she focused on developing her divine gift.

And now she is a psychologist helping other highly sensitive people to accept their gift of empathy, overcome their fears and depression, and learn how to decrease their sensitivity to succeed in all spheres of their life. Moreover, Helena wrote a guide for empaths where she explains what they should do to survive in the modern world.

Introduction

In today's hectic world that is brimming with opportunities, everyone feels overloaded with information and exhausted from the never-ending pursuit of happiness and success. As a result, some people succeed in life, while others live in extreme poverty and suffer from poor physical and mental health. The more negative emotions they experience, the more miserable they feel. They may be kind-hearted, more talented than their successful friends and acquaintances, but they are too vulnerable. Sometimes such people may feel like aliens who don't belong to this planet. They feel detached from this world. They often suffer from loneliness, depression and anxiety, and these negative emotions and destructive thoughts block their way to happiness.

Have you ever felt that way? If so, then you may be sure that you are a highly sensitive person, or an empath. Such people are able to perceive both negative and positive emotions of others. Being an empath is not a curse, it is just the way of perceiving the world on a deeper emotional level. All highly sensitive people are very creative, compassionate and observant. Moreover, they understand other people's needs and try to help them. Such is their predestination.

In this book you will learn about types of highly sensitive people, find out if you are one of them, and learn how to survive and thrive in this world being a highly sensitive person.

I. Types of Highly Sensitive People

In this section, you will find out what is the nature of highly sensitive people. You will also learn the difference between Empaths, Intuitives, Psychics and Healers.

1. Highly Sensitive People (HSPs)

About 20 percent of the inhabitants of our planet can be rightly called 'Highly sensitive people'. In most cases, such people are born with these psychic abilities. Highly sensitive people have an intense reaction to positive and negative events that take place in this world. For that reason, they can be overwhelmed by stressful situations, or even loud noises. HSPs are more compassionate, more attentive to their environment and other people's opinions. They are vulnerable, they can cry easily since they process all incoming information on a deeper emotional level. As a rule, highly sensitive people can be therapists or artists.

Traits of Highly Sensitive People

Let's look at the common traits of highly sensitive people in more detail:

1. They feel deeply

One of the main traits of highly sensitive people is their ability to sense everything more deeply compared to less sensitive people. They are often guided by intuition.

2. They express more intense emotions

Highly sensitive people show more empathy in certain situations. For example, they will be more concerned about other people's problems.

3. They avoid team sports

As a rule, highly sensitive people try to avoid team sports since they do not like being watched by everyone. Instead, they choose individual sports (such as running, or bicycling).

4. They don't make hasty decisions

Before making any decisions, highly sensitive people always consider all details. For that reason, it is harder for them to make the right decision at once compared to other less sensitive people.

5. They are observant

Highly sensitive people tend to pay attention to all the details. For example, they will notice a new purse that their friend is wearing, or feel when the weather is changing.

6. They enjoy working from home or being self-employed

Highly sensitive people are usually self-employed, or they enjoy working from home because they can control external stimuli. For those highly sensitive people who have to work in an office with a lot of people, an office cubicle is the best option.

7. They tend to suffer from depression and anxiety

Highly sensitive people may often suffer from depression or anxiety, especially after having several bad experiences in life. As a result, they do not feel secure. However, highly sensitive people living in a supportive environment may not feel anxious or depressed.

8. They can't stand loud noise

Highly sensitive people cannot stand noise (e.g. loud talking, or phone ringing), which may overstimulate their sensitive nervous system, and lead to extreme irritation.

9. They can't watch violent and horror movies

Since highly sensitive people are too emotional, horror or violent movies may make them anxious, and even cause insomnia and lead to nightmares.

10. They cry more easily and sensitive to criticism

Highly sensitive people can cry easily when their friends or colleagues make them feel guilty or embarrassed. They take every reproach as a personal insult. In addition, such people are sensitive to criticism compared with less sensitive people. It is hard for them to hear something negative.

2. Empaths

Empaths are highly sensitive people that feel emotions of people around them as their own. If your friend is angry, you may feel angry too without any reason. If someone feels sad, you may start feeling sad (depressed) as well. In other words, empaths can scan other people's energy. Empaths possess an innate ability to feel other's emotions.

Empaths can read other people's thoughts, and perceive their emotional state. They may even feel chronic fatigue or unexplained pain every day due to emotional overload. In other words, they accumulate the energy and emotions of this world. Empaths attract people by their energy.

Traits of Empaths

Let's look at the common traits of empaths in more detail:

1. Being in public places can be a real torture for them

If empaths find themselves in crowded places (such as stadiums, concert halls or supermarkets), they can experience the whole gamut of emotions coming from other people. These emotions may range from despair to joy.

2. Feeling others' emotions and taking them on as their own

As a rule, empaths can perceive emotions of people nearby. Some of them can feel emotions of people who are far away. Moreover, advanced empaths may know when others are having bad thoughts about them, even if those people discussing them live in another country.

3. They can't watch violence and tragedy on the TV

Since empaths are too sensitive, it is unbearable for them to watch news, violent movies, and TV shows with cruelty scenes because such negative flow of information will cause anxiety or depression in them.

4. They know when somebody lies

Empaths know if their friends or relatives lie to them. They may feel what the speaker is feeling in the moment of conversation. In some cases, his/her feelings may contradict their words. But empaths will feel this contradiction.

5. They take on physical symptoms from others

If you are an empath, and your close friend or relative has headache, or has contracted a disease (e.g. an eye infection), you may start suffering from the same symptoms.

6. They feel constant fatigue

Empaths feel constant fatigue since they lose a lot of energy, even from taking too much from other people, who try to offload their problems on empaths. For that reason, a lot of empaths suffer from chronic fatigue syndrome.

7. They show interest in healing, holistic medicine and supernatural things

Many empaths show interest in alternative medicine and supernatural things. They go to lectures and read books to know more about alternative ways of healing and supernatural things.

8. They are very creative

Many empaths enjoy acting, singing, drawing, dancing, or writing. They try to express their creative energy through these activities.

9. They love nature and animals

Empaths love nature and animals. As a rule, their job is somehow connected with nature or animals. A lot of volunteers are empaths who are aimed at helping other people for free.

10. They need solitude

Empaths need to spend some time on their own to restore their lost energy, otherwise they may go crazy.

11. They hate doing things they don't like

Empaths hate doing something they don't like. If they have to do something against their will, they will feel unhappy. As a result, they may fall sick.

12. They always search for answers

Their inquisitive mind always searches for answers to questions. Moreover, they possess the thirst for knowledge which they try to quench in every possible way.

13. They enjoy freedom, but dislike routine

Empaths enjoy freedom, but hate rules and routine. They don't like being controlled since they are afraid of losing their freedom. The thought itself is just unbearable for them.

14. They disdain clutter

Empaths disdain clutter. It makes them feel worried, which results in blocking the energy flow. They feel more comfortable in a tidy room.

15. They enjoy daydreaming

Empaths can spend hours in their dream world where they can feel safe and sound. If their life is not really eventful, empaths will spend more time in their virtual reality. They can be anywhere in their thoughts detached from this physical reality.

16. They often see vivid or lucid dreams
Empaths can see vivid and lucid dreams. Moreover, they pay attention to their dream content. They believe that their dreams are connected to their physical reality. They even try to figure out the meaning of their dreams.

17. They are excellent listeners

Empaths don't expand on themselves until they start trusting someone. However, they enjoy learning about others. Complete strangers often pour out their hearts to these highly sensitive people. They feel subconsciously that empaths would listen to them with compassion.

18. They are intolerant of narcissism

Empaths are kind-hearted and try to be often tolerant of other people. The character trait that they don't like about others is egocentrism. Empaths can't be around such people for too long, otherwise they may lose their temper.

19. They do not like to buy second-hand goods or antiques

Empaths will never buy antiques or second-hand goods because they can feel the negative energy of previous owners absorbed by these objects. For that reason, they prefer to acquire new things even if they are more expensive.

20. They can experience changes in mood

As a rule, most empaths experience mood swings. One moment they can be full of joy and suddenly they may burst into tears for no reason at all.

3. Intuitives

Intuition plays an important role in lives of many people, especially highly sensitive ones. Some of them use it every day without even realizing it. Their intuition is manifested through sudden bright ideas, inspiration, apprehensions, and so on.

In most cases, intuitive people know about their gift, and try to listen to their inner voice, which helps them find answers to their questions and then make the right decisions. Moreover, they can help other people resolve their problems.

Traits of Intuitives

Let's look at the common traits of intuitives in more detail:

1. They are guided by the inner voice

All intuitive people listen to the voice of intuition which helps them make important decisions at the crucial moments of their lives. All creative people are also guided by intuition.

2. They need to spend their time in solitude

All intuitive people need to spend some time in solitude since it is impossible to hear a low voice of intuition in noisy, crowded places. In most cases, they will be able to hear their inner voice in silence.

3. They connect deeply with others

Intuitives feel an invisible, deep connection to the whole world. When they watch their favorite singers perform on television, they can feel their emotions as if they are at the concert. They feel both positive (such as joy, happiness) and negative emotions (such as guilt, disgust, pride, or embarrassment) simply by watching others.

4. They always pay attention to their dreams

Intuitives tend to pay attention to their dreams, which help them to connect with their unconscious mind and find answers to their questions.

5. They are drawn to unconventional things

Intuitives are always drawn to unconventional and abnormal things. In their search of new knowledge, such people always look for new concepts in all spheres of life.

6. They socialize selectively

Intuitive people are reluctant to mix with strangers. They prefer loneliness to a bad company. However, if they meet the like-minded people, they will easily start a conversation that could flow endlessly.

4. Psychics (Clairvoyants, Clairaudients, Mediums)

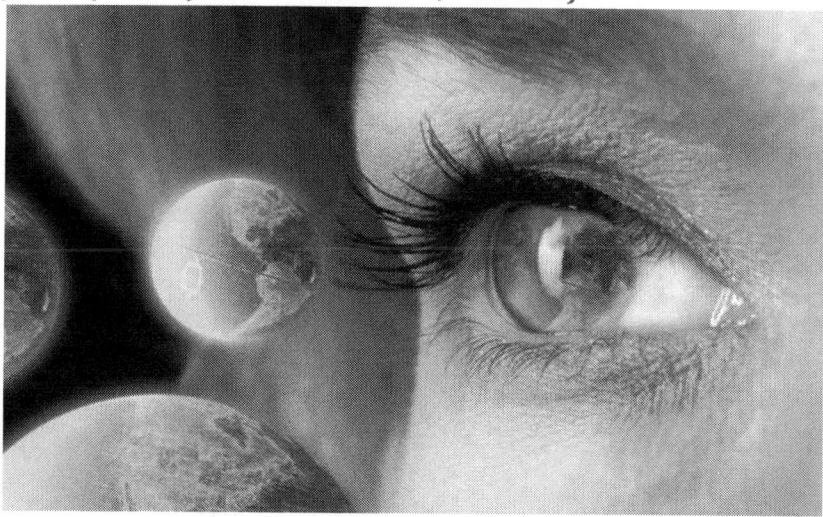

Psychics are open to the information that other people cannot perceive. Psychics (clairvoyants, clairaudients and mediums) can receive information about people, objects, events, and places through extrasensory perception.

1. Clairvoyants
These highly sensitive people can tell about the past, see what is going on at present somewhere in the distance, predict future events, and find missing people.

2. Clairaudients
These psychics are able to hear voices from their guardian angels and spirits. They receive the information by hearing answers to their questions from the spirit world.

3. Mediums
Mediums are also psychics who can talk to spirits since they are able to perceive their high-frequency vibrations. They receive all the necessary information directly from the spirit world.

5. Spiritual (Energy) Healers

In addition to empaths, intuitives, psychics, there is also a type of highly sensitive people called healers. Such people can heal themselves, and heal others. However, some of them do not know that they have the gift of healing, but they keep healing other people with their positive energy without even realizing it.

Let's look at the common traits of spiritual healers:

1. They are very sensitive
They may feel fear, chronic pain (such as low back pain) or suffer from headaches, autoimmune disorders, or digestive issues. They can also perceive, hear and see things other people can't. Healers can feel other people's moods. They know when somebody is angry or upset. In addition, healers often see vivid dreams connected with their past or future.

2. They are introverts and enjoy solitude
Healers are introverts who enjoy spending some time in solitude to restore their lost energy. They always feel exhausted after spending time at a party or a concert.

3. They help others
They often work as nurses or physicians because they enjoy helping others. People always feel better close to healers. Complete strangers are willing to pour out their hearts to them since they feel subconsciously that these people possess healing energy. Animals and kids are often drawn to healers since they feel safe near them.

4. They show interest in healing art

They are interested in a variety of healing methods (such as reiki or ayurveda). They also like to go to medical lectures and read medical books to learn more about alternative ways of healing. Moreover, some of them work as psychologists, massage therapists, physical therapists, doctors, or nurses.

5. Drugs affect them differently

When it comes to healers, drugs may affect them differently or have no effect at all. However, natural remedies like herbs may have a beneficial effect on their health.

II. Emotional Sensitivity Tests

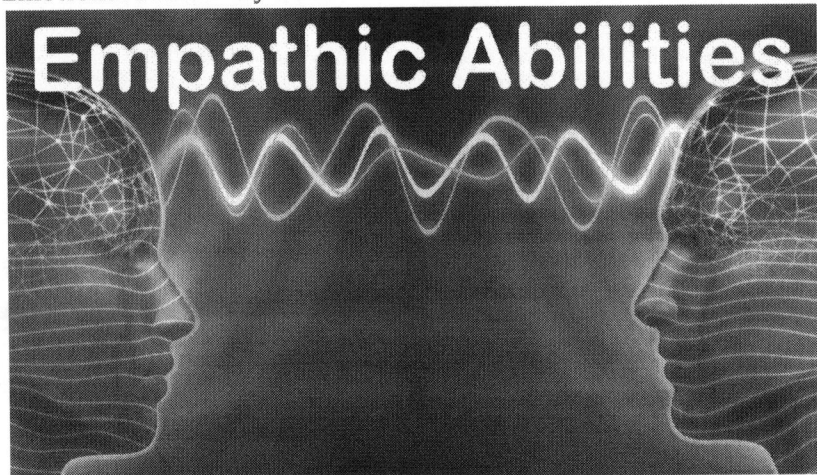

In this section you will find several tests that can be used to define whether you are a highly sensitive person, empath, intuitive, or spiritual healer. All you have to do is answer several questions included in the tests. You can take all of these tests, or choose only some of them. After realizing who you are in this world, you will start learning how to control your emotions so you can enjoy your life to the fullest.

1) Emotional Sensitivity Self-Assessment Test

Answer all of these questions. Circle the questions that are true for you. The more circled questions you have, the more likely you are a highly sensitive person.

Yes 1. You are often told by your friends and relatives that you are too sensitive.

2. You are often afraid that you can hurt other people's feelings.

3. If your friends ask you where you would like to go with them, and you choose the place where your friends would like to go (in your opinion) because you want to please them.

No 4. It is hard for you to make any decisions.

5. If unfair things happen, it is hard for you to let the situation go.

6. By spending some time outdoors and admiring beautiful landscapes, you feel calmer.

7. When other people around you are upset or angry, you also feel upset or angry.

8. You try to hide your own emotions.

9. You try to fit in with other people.

10. If your friend does not return your call, you think she (he) is angry with you.

11. You react more intensely to bad news on TV than the rest of people.

12. When you are worried, you are not able to think clearly.

13. You don't want to take part in social activities because you are afraid of being criticized.

14. You often refuse to go out with your friends since you don't feel like going to noisy, crowded places.

15. You may eat, work or sleep too much.

16. You sometimes can't figure out why you are feeling a certain way.

17. You believe that other people try to make your life more complicated.

18. You always wonder why other people want to be around you.

19. You are afraid of changes.

20. You hate yourself for being too emotional.

Scoring:

If you have answered more than 14 questions as 'true', then you are an empath. If have answered more than 10 questions as 'true' of yourself, then you are a highly sensitive person.

2) Are You a Spiritual Healer?

Answer all of these questions following your inner voice. Circle the questions that are true for you. The more circled questions you have, the more likely you are a spiritual healer.

1. Do the light bulbs often burn out in your presence?

2. Can you feel the emotions of other people?

3. Do you perceive the mood of other people when you enter the room?

4. Do you have an odd reaction to certain drugs?

5. Do you attract children and animals like a magnet?

6. Do you suffer from headaches, autoimmune disorders, or digestive issues?

7. Do you often see vivid dreams connected with your past or future?

8. Do you like spending some time in solitude?

9. Do you often help other people?

10. Do you show interest in alternative medicine? Do you visit medical lectures? Do you read medical books?

3) Are You Highly Sensitive?

Answer all of these questions following your inner voice. Circle the questions that are true for you. The more circled questions you have, the more likely you are a highly sensitive person.

1. You are easily overwhelmed by strong emotions of other people.

2. You can feel and notice even the slightest changes in your environment.

3. You can feel other people's moods which affect you.

4. You are very sensitive to pain.

5. You desperately need to withdraw to any place where you will be able to spend some time on your own to relax and get rid of negative emotions that you have absorbed from other people.

6. You are very sensitive to caffeine.

7. You are easily affected by strong smells, bright lights, or loud noise nearby.

8. You have a rich inner world.

9. You adore listening to beautiful music.

10. You are conscientious.

11. You can startle easily.

12. You get nervous if you have to do too many things at once.

13. You do your best to avoid making any mistakes and try not to forget anything.

14. You do not like watching violent movies on TV and try to avoid it.

15. You get too annoyed if find yourself in a crowd at a stadium, or a concert where there are a lot of people around you.

16. If you are very hungry, this has an adverse effect on your mood and leads to lack of concentration.

17. Any changes in your life are stressful for you.

18. You tend to smell delicate scents, enjoy fine works of art, and enjoy delicate tastes of dishes.

19. You feel overwhelmed by emotions when a lot of things are going on in your life at once.

20. You do your best to avoid upsetting situations in your life.

21. When you are observed while completing a task, you may get too nervous and perform your work much worse than usual.

22. When you were a child, you were considered too shy and sensitive.

Scoring:
If you have answered more than 15 questions as 'true', then you are an empath. If you have answered more than 11 questions as 'true' of yourself, then you are a highly sensitive person.

4) Are You An Empath?

Answer all of these questions. Circle the questions that are true for you. The more circled questions you have, the more likely you are an empath.

1. Do you often search for answers that torture your mind?

2. Do you often experience other people's pain?

3. Do you love animals?

4. Do you read other people's thoughts?

5. Do you enjoy solitude?

6. Do you help others when they ask you for help?

7. Can you cry easily while you are watching movies with tragedy scenes?

8. Are you in harmony with nature?

9. Are you a good listener?

10. Do you have a bent for music? Are you creative?

5) How Intuitive Are You?

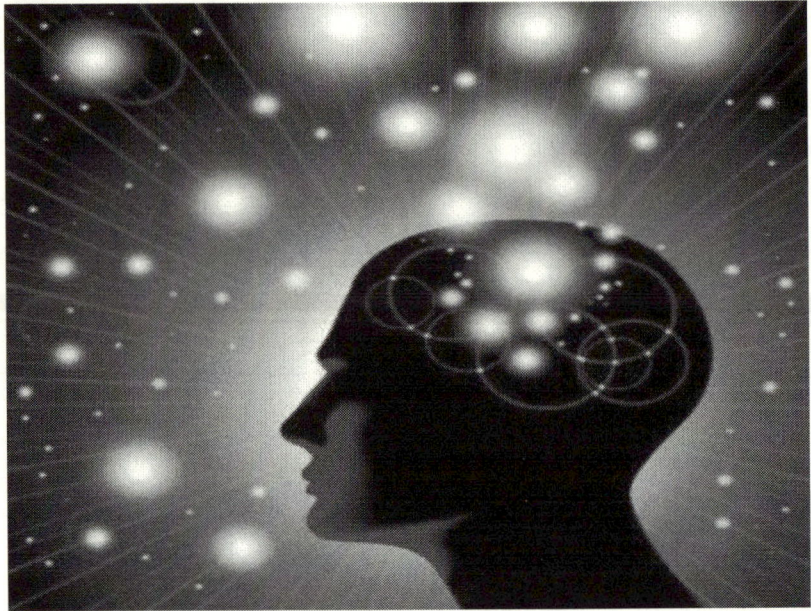

This quiz can help you find out how much you are using your intuition. Answer all of these questions following your inner voice. Circle the questions that are true for you. The more circled questions you have, the more likely you are intuitive.

1. When you don't have a ready answer, you are

A. patient.

B. worried.

2. In difficult situations, you stay highly motivated

A. most of the time.

B. sometimes.

3. When you are working on a difficult problem, you try to

A. find the right solution.

B. play around with possibilities.

4. When you don't agree completely with your friend or colleague, you always try to

A. let him (her) know about it.

B. keep silent about your disagreement.

5. While working on a task, you change your tactics

A. rarely.

B. frequently.

6. You prefer to be told

A. how to perform a task in detail.

B. only what should be done.

7. When things become very complicated, you

A. start feeling happy and excited.

B. start feeling uncertain.

8. As a general rule,

A. changes make you nervous.

B. you are glad to unexpected changes.

9. Your reading preferences include

A. a variety of genres (including fiction).

B. only job-related materials.

10. If your opinion differs from the experts, you

A. usually keep to your beliefs.

B. can't ignore authority.

11. When you have to perform several tasks, you

A. deal with them simultaneously.

B. accomplish one task and then start performing another.

12. When learning new things, you

A. acquire complete knowledge first.

B. start practicing without learning the rules.

13. Unpredictable people are

A. irritating.

B. interesting.

14. At school you are (were) better at

A. *giving detailed answers.*

B. *giving short answers.*

15. When you make a mistake, you tend to

A. *notice it.*

B. *ignore it.*

16. When giving an explanation, you are more likely to

A. *draw an analogy.*

B. *rely upon figures.*

17. When making a decision, you only listen to

A. *the voice of reason.*

B. *the voice of your heart.*

18. When you are wrong, you

A. *confess it.*

B. *justify yourself.*

19. When you are faced with a dilemma, you will try to

A. *ask for advice.*

B. *resolve it yourself.*

20. While working on a project, you prefer to

A. *work according to a prearranged schedule.*

B. *work on your own schedule.*

21. When you make an appointment for the next week, you might say

A. *"Let's fix an exact time right now."*

B. *"Please, call me the day before."*

22. You are considered by your friends and colleagues as

A. *a person who generates new ideas.*

B. *a person who performs a task considering all details.*

Scoring:

If you have circled 'A' on the following questions: 1, 2, 4, 7, 9, 10, 11, 14, 16, 18, and 22, give yourself 1 point.

If you have circled 'B' on the following questions: 3, 5, 6, 8, 12, 13, 15, 17, 19, 20, and 21, give yourself 1 point.

If you have scored more than 16 points, you always listen to the voice of your intuition when solving problems and making decisions. In all likelihood, you are a highly intuitive person.

If you have scored less than 15 points, you use your intuition more than an analytic mind.

If you have scored less than 9 points, you sometimes use your intuition. However, in most cases, you prefer using your an analytic mind, which is more important to you. In this case, your intuition may be a poor adviser.

If you have scored less than 5 points, you mostly use a rational approach to making decisions and solving problems. In all likelihood, you do not really trust your inner voice.

III. Survival Tips for Highly Sensitive People and Empaths

Feeling other people's emotions is very exhausting for highly sensitive people. For that reason, many of them feel drained of energy, which can lead to poor health without proper care.

Here are the useful tips that will help all highly sensitive people and empaths cope with their sensitivity and make the most of it:

1. Realize your gift and accept it

Sensitive people are aimed at helping others. And only then they start thinking about themselves. The weight of emotions received from other people can make their lives really unbearable. However, there are several rules that should be followed to minimize the consequences of this sensitivity. First of all, you should accept your gift. This is not a disease. This is your personality trait. You were born with it. This is the way you feel this world. After realizing this, you will feel relieved because mindfulness is already a half-way to the solution to any problem. Being an empath is not the end of the world. You are not an outcast of society. Do not listen to negative opinions of other people in regard to your gift. Remember one thing, 'You are amazing. You are intuitive, creative and compassionate. You have a rich inner world'. These are the gifts which other less sensitive people could only dream about.

2. Do not suppress your sensitivity

A lot of empaths try to suppress their sensitivity to stop feeling emotions of other people. This total self-protection will tell on their mental and physical health sooner or later. What is more, it will affect their career, relationships, etc.

3. Do not criticize yourself

All highly sensitive people tend to criticize themselves more than they could criticize others. You should treat yourself with compassion and try to listen to your inner critic with patience. Control the thoughts by focusing on positive thoughts that will bring you comfort and joy. First of all, you should acknowledge the negative thoughts and then they will go away.

4. Be thankful for your gift

Now that you know you possess your gift, you should thank your stars for this. You are one of those people who can experience all the depth of emotions (such as joy, or love). By expressing sincere gratitude for your gifts, you activate a positive energy and fill your life space with it. As soon as you learn how to manage your gift, you will make the most of it.

5. Search for kindred spirits

At first you may feel lonely and detached from this world. But you are not alone. There are many the like-minded souls searching for someone like you to speak out, because they know that you will listen to them, and they will listen to you and support you. Hang out with advanced empaths as much as possible. You will only benefit from this. They already know how to control their gifts. In addition, they will help you use your powers by sharing their wisdom with you. Such support will enhance your self-esteem.

6. Pay attention to the source of your thoughts

All highly sensitive people should figure out the source of their thoughts, especially negatives ones. Ask yourself why you are feeling sad at this moment, and if you see that there is no reason for you to feel this way, then this is not your emotion. After mastering this skill, you will be able to search for the right solution. For example, you will be able to avoid visiting crowded places, or hanging out with unpleasant people that irritate you. Instead, it is more advisable to use your spare time for doing things that will restore your vital energy.

7. View the situation from another perspective

However, if you have to deal with unpleasant people, try to view the situation from another perspective. For example, you can ask yourself why he (she) is acting this way. Maybe he (she) acts this way because of his (her) trauma he (she) suffered in the past. By changing your point of view towards these people, you will be able to understand them and forgive them. As a result, you will stop feeling angry at them and will minimize their influence on your mind and body. Moreover, you may start feeling sympathy for them. By getting rid of past insults, you will get rid of negative emotions that have accumulated in your soul.

8. Create a shield

There are important meetings, family reunions and other social events where highly sensitive people will feel out of their element. Too many people, too many emotions. All this can cause emotional overload. And all empaths have to learn how to deal with such situations. For example, you can form an energy shield. This mental barrier will help you block the negative energy coming from other people. Or you can create an energy bubble made of light that will surround you when you start feeling negative vibrations from the environment. In the middle of the bubble, you will feel safe and protected because you have left all the negative emotions on the outside.

9. Cleanse your chakras

Chakras are the energy centers in the human body which are responsible for your physical and mental health. For that reason, it is very important to keep them free from negative energy. First of all, you can use the sage burning technique, which is quite effective in counteracting the negative vibrations. All you have to do is burn sage and its scent will help you cleanse all the chakras and prevent them from the blockage. The flame will absorb all the negativity around you.

You can also take a sea salt foot bath which will not only soothe the pain in your tired feet, but also cleanse your chakras from the negative energy. All you have to do is immerse your feet in warm water for 10 minutes.

10. Repeat positive affirmations

Though empaths are very open and kind-hearted people, but it is hard for them to remain positive since they tend to absorb foreign energy (ranging from anger to sadness) and suffer from it. To maintain positive attitude towards yourself and life, it is advisable to repeat positive affirmations on a daily basis (in the morning or in the evening) and they will fill you with confidence and increase your self-esteem.

11. Spend some time on your own in a cozy, quiet place

All empaths need to spend some time on their own, especially if they live with others. It should be a cozy, quiet place (such as a bedroom, study, or bathroom) where they will be able to relax and have a rest from irritating noise. In addition, they can listen to relaxing music, or play Tibetan singing bowls, which are great for cleansing the mind from the negative energy.

Being in this secluded room, don't watch TV and don't talk on the phone. At this moment you should focus only on yourself. You are the center of your own universe. Let this place be the place where you will be able to restore your lost energy and improve your wellbeing.

12. Get things done in off-peak hours

It is hard for all highly sensitive people to work in standard hours. If you have to work in the morning, then you should try to get up earlier than usual. This way, you will be able to enjoy the silence and manage to get things done before your family wakes up. For example, you will have more time which you could spend on mediation or doing yoga, or repeating positive affirmations.

Ideally, empaths should work and spend their spare time in off-peak hours to avoid stress that could be caused by loud noise (coming from crowds, or heavy traffic on the roads). For example, you could go to movies on weekdays instead of weekends, and eat in cafes or restaurants in off-peak hours.

In addition, before going to bed, you should turn off your mobile phone and TV set, and then you can read an uplifting book, or listen to relaxing music.

13. Contemplate things pleasant to the eye

Since empaths are too sensitive, the surroundings affect their health to a great extent. For that reason, they should try to decorate their homes with things that can please their eye. By contemplating a beautiful picture hanging on the wall, you will fill yourself with positive energy of joy and feel your mind with serenity.

14. Spend more time outdoors

Nature is a great healer for all empaths. By spending some time in the country, you will be able to replenish the lost energy and improve your physical and mental health. By admiring the breathtaking landscapes, you will be able to calm your restless mind. But if you don't have time to go to the country, just look out of the window to enjoy the fascinating beauty of the starry sky. By looking into the endless depths of the universe, you will feel the unity with the whole world. And soon all worries that have tortured your soul will go away. Stargazing is akin the meditation that helps improve your mental health.

15. Eat only healthy food

Highly sensitive people may suffer not only from the negative surroundings. They also suffer from unhealthy food, which has an adverse effect on their health. If they eat junk food, then they will feel bad. That is why it is so important for all empaths to keep to a healthy and well-balanced diet. They should consume fresh vegetables and fruit, as well as meat, fish and legumes. However, they can indulge in sweets (but in moderation) to keep their blood sugar steady.

Empaths should not omit the meals since extreme hunger may be detrimental to their physical and mental health. In addition, all empaths are sensitive to caffeine. Coffee, tea and chocolate contain a lot of caffeine which stimulates nervous system. If you limit the caffeine intake, then you will feel calmer.

16. Practice yoga and meditation, and do gentle exercises

It is highly advisable for all empaths to do gentle exercises, go jogging or walk in a park, practice tai chi, hatha yoga or meditation. These activities will strengthen their immunity and nervous system, as well as improve their overall health. Those empaths who enjoy going to the gym should exercise before 7 pm to let their nervous system calm down before they go to bed because this process will take several hours.

17. Get enough sleep

Lack of sleep (less than 7-8 hours) may cause mood swings, irritability, and lack of concentration. Lack of sleep can worsen the physical and mental health of highly sensitive people making them aggressive and exhausted, and decrease their immunity. For that reason, sleep plays an important role in the wellbeing of all people, especially empaths.

18. Wear noise-cancelling headphones

Highly sensitive people are too sensitive to loud noise. That is why they should wear noise-reducing headphones which will protect them from unbearably loud sounds. Thus, they will be able to keep their composure in noisy, crowded places, which they have to visit from time to time.

19. Use crystals and stones to protect yourself from negative energy

For ages, stones and crystals have been applied to balance the energy in all chakras and to protect their owner from illnesses and misfortunes.

The following stones and crystals can protect all highly sensitive people from any negative vibrations:

Quartz crystals
Quartz crystals have healing, protective and energizing properties.

34

Amethyst
Amethyst can be used for protection and healing. It also reduces anxiety.

Rose Quartz
Rose Quartz brings its owner emotional healing and love.

Obsidian
Obsidian has protective properties.

Black tourmaline
Black tourmaline can protect all highly sensitive people from the negative vibrations around them.

20. Deep breathing technique
Deep breathing exercises can help all highly sensitive people to calm down in the most stressful situations which they can't escape because they have to be present at a business meeting to discuss certain problems of the company. For example, when your business partner is saying something that makes you feel nervous, do not panic. First of all, you should realize that these are not your own emotions. Next, try to take a deep breath before reacting to his (her) words. Such tactics will help you gain time, and calm down. As a result, you will be able to think what should be said and done next. Take a deep breath again, and give your answer.

Such technique can be used in any stressful situations, at work, at home, or in noisy, crowded places when you start feeling anxious. Deep breathing technique will help you get rid of negative emotions and feelings fast and easily. What is more, you will be able to restore your energy balance and improve your mood.

IV. The Eating Plan for Empaths and Highly Sensitive People

All empaths often catch colds and flu as well as other ailments because they absorb the negative energy of other people added to their own thoughts and emotions. However, some empaths get used to feeling bad, and may not understand that their health is affected by others. As a result, their health gradually becomes weaker.

When you feel lousy, you want to eat junk food and food that contains a lot of sugar because it will help you feel more energetic for a short period of time. But soon you will feel hungry and emotionally exhausted again because fast food is low in nutrients. These substances (including protein, vitamins and minerals) are essential for strong immune system which protects the body from infections and illnesses.

Processed foods containing chemicals have a detrimental effect on the whole body, including the hormone system and mental health (causing phobias and mood swings, and increasing emotional sensitivity).

All empaths should follow a healthy diet, which is rich in protein, vitamins and minerals. If your diet is low in all the necessary nutrients, it is advisable to take high-quality vitamin and mineral supplements containing vitamin C, B vitamins, and zinc (if you often catch colds). By avoiding junk food and eating healthy foods, you will improve your health, increase your energy level and decrease your sensitivity.

V. Aromatherapy for Empaths and Highly Sensitive People

As it was mentioned above, all empaths absorb other people's energies and emotions, both negative and positive. Empaths should work on themselves more than other people in today's world overfilled with negative vibrations. It is the primary task for all highly sensitive people to protect themselves from other people's unpleasant feelings and emotions which may cause emotional overload in them. Aromatherapy is one of the best ways of energetic self-protection and relaxation.

Aromatherapy is an alternative medicine that is aimed at healing the mind and body applying essential oils extracted from resin and plants.

Essential oils were already used by the ancient Egyptians in 4500 BC for healing and religious rites. Aromatherapy helps ease pain, reduce stress and anxiety, improve mood, increase energy level, and even treat insomnia.

Essential oils can be used in a vaporizer, foot and hand baths, massage, and inhalations. You can also apply them on your pillow or a handkerchief. They will help you create a relaxing atmosphere in the room before going to bed or practicing meditation.

Essential oils are very concentrated. For that reason, they should be diluted with a carrier oil (such as almond oil, jojoba oil, grapeseed oil, olive oil, or wheatgerm oil), and applied only in small amounts to avoid irritation and allergic reactions.

The most popular essential oils for highly sensitive people and empaths

Here is a list of the most popular essential oils that are just perfect for all empaths and highly sensitive people since they have a lot of healing properties. These essential oils will help you relieve chronic pain, reduce anxiety, charge you with energy, as well as improve your physical and mental health.

Basil essential oil

In ancient times, basil was used to scare away evil spirits. This essential oil is perfect for anxiety, sleeplessness, tiredness and depression. This essential oil has uplifting and relaxing properties. It can be used for foot baths, massage, and inhalations. Sprinkle 2-3 drops on the pillow or a handkerchief and you will get rid of headache.

Chamomile essential oil

Chamomile essential oil is excellent for stress, insomnia, and headaches thanks to its calming properties. Add several drops of this essential oil on the pillow before going to bed or before taking a bath. But at first you should dilute it with a carrier oil.

Frankincense essential oil

Frankincense essential oil is used for massage, baths, and inhalation. You can massage your temples using this oil to ease your headache. Frankincense has calming and uplifting properties. It clears the mind, reduces anxiety, and improves mood. Moreover, it is great for tiredness and emotional disorders.

Geranium essential oil

This essential oil has both uplifting, and energizing properties, as well as soothing and sleep-inducing effect. It is just perfect for alleviating the symptoms of depression. Geranium is great for restoring the energy balance. By adding one drop of this essential oil to a hot foot bath, you will feel complete relaxation and serenity. By adding a drop of geranium oil to a cool foot bath, you will feel energetic and refreshed.

Jasmine essential oil

Jasmine has both uplifting and calming effect. It helps restore the energy balance, and relieves anxiety. It is great for depression, tiredness, irritability, and stress. Its aroma makes you feel optimistic.

Lavender essential oil

In addition to its antiseptic and antibacterial properties, lavender essential oil has a relaxing and uplifting effect on highly sensitive people. Its aroma is great for fatigue and depression. To relieve anxiety, all you have to do is add several drops of this oil to a hot foot bath, and soon you will feel relaxed. By adding a few drops of lavender oil to a cool foot bath, you will feel more energetic.

Neroli essential oil

Neroli essential oil has calming and sleep-inducing effect. It is also good for depression, fears, anxiety, overexcitement and stress. Moreover, it restores the energy balance. It is great for relaxing bath or massage. It can also be used for inhalation. Just sprinkle a few drops of this wonderful essential oil on the pillow or handkerchief, and you will feel happy.

Peppermint essential oil

Peppermint essential oil has soothing and cooling properties. It is great for clearing the head and relieving mental fatigue, nausea and cold. It can be used for massage, inhalation and baths.

Rose essential oil

Rose essential oil has uplifting and antidepressant effect. It also relieves fatigue and clears the head. It can be used for massage and baths. To restore your lost energy and relieve headache, all you have to do is add 10 drops of rose oil to the hot water and take a bath.

Clary sage essential oil

In ancient times, clary sage essential oil was used for healing all nervous problems. The oil has both soothing and uplifting properties. It is good for sleeplessness, depression, tiredness, anxiety, and headaches. It can be used for baths and massage.

Valerian essential oil

Valerian essential oil is good for insomnia, irritability, tension, and mood swings. It has calming and soporific properties. It can be used for massage, inhalation and baths. A few drops of the valerian oil on your pillow will help you calm down and sleep well.

Ylang-ylang essential oil

Thanks to its relaxing effect, ylang-ylang is good for anxiety, stress, tension, sleeplessness and depression. It can be used for baths, inhalation and massage. However, it should be used in moderation, since it has a potent smell.

The most effective essential oils for anxiety, depression, fatigue and stress

All empaths tend to feel anxious, tired, stressed and depressed which is mostly caused by the absorption of other people's feelings and emotions, both negative and positive. This may result in emotional overload which manifests itself through tense muscles, chronic lumbar pain, chronic headaches, indigestion and insomnia. In this case, it is advisable to apply essential oils which will help relieve these symptoms by calming the nervous system.

Anxiety

The main symptoms of anxiety are chronic headaches, insomnia, and muscle tension. Aromatherapy is one of the most effective remedies for anxiety since a pleasant and relaxing aroma of essential oils helps alleviate the symptoms of this condition.

The best essential oils which can be used to relieve anxiety:
- Bergamot oil (uplifting, refreshing, stress-relieving)
- Frankincense oil (relaxing, calming, uplifting)
- Jasmine oil (uplifting, calming)
- Lavender oil (uplifting, relaxing, relieving tension)
- Mandarin oil (relaxing, sleep-inducing)
- Neroli oil (sleep-inducing, calming)
- Rosewood oil (calming, relaxing)
- Sandalwood oil (sleep-inducing, stress-relieving, relaxing)
- Spruce oil (soothing, relaxing)
- Valerian oil (calming, sleep-inducing)
- Ylang-ylang oil (relaxing, stress-relieving, uplifting)

Depression

The main symptoms of depression are sleeplessness, melancholy and apathy. By using the essential oils, you will be able to improve your mood and alleviate other symptoms of depression.

The best essential oils that can be used to relieve the symptoms of depression:

- Bergamot oil (uplifting, refreshing, antidepressant, stress-relieving)
- Clary sage oil (relaxing, uplifting)
- Frankincense oil (relaxing, calming, uplifting, relieving anxiety)
- Geranium oil (uplifting, relaxing, sleep-inducing, invigorating)
- Jasmine oil (uplifting, stress-relieving, calming)
- Lavender oil (uplifting, calming, relieving tension)
- Neroli oil (antidepressant, sleep-inducing, relaxing)
- Rose oil (uplifting, antidepressant, energizing)
- Rosewood oil (relaxing, calming)
- Sandalwood oil (sleep-inducing, relaxing, stress-relieving)
- Ylang-ylang oil (relaxing, stress-relieving, uplifting)

Fatigue

Fatigue is caused by stress and emotional overload. Essential oils are excellent for relieving the symptoms of tiredness since they possess calming and energizing properties.

The best essential oils which can be applied for relieving the symptoms of fatigue:

- Bergamot oil (uplifting, refreshing, antidepressant, stress-relieving)
- Clary sage oil (relaxing, uplifting)
- Eucalyptus oil (calming, pain-relieving)
- Frankincense oil (relaxing, calming, uplifting, relieving anxiety)
- Geranium oil (uplifting, soothing, sleep-inducing, energizing)
- Jasmine oil (uplifting, antidepressant, calming, stress-relieving)
- Lavender oil (uplifting, relaxing, antidepressant, relieving tension)
- Lemon oil (energizing, invigorating, clearing the head, relieving mental fatigue)
- Peppermint oil (cooling, calming, clearing the head, relieving mental fatigue)

Stress

Unfortunately, empaths tend to suffer from stress more than less sensitive people. However, not all of them can cope with it, which results in chronic stress. Its main symptoms are anxiety, muscle pain, allergy, insomnia, depression, and mood swings. Such condition may cause serious illnesses, if not treated in time. In this case, aromatherapy is great for relieving the symptoms of chronic stress, thanks to the uplifting, soporific, and relaxing properties of essential oils.

The best essential oils that can be applied to relieve the symptoms of (chronic) stress:

- Basil oil (relaxing, uplifting, easing headache)
- Bergamot oil (uplifting, stress-relieving, refreshing)

- Chamomile oil (stress-relieving, calming, sleep-inducing, relieving headache)
- Clary sage oil (relaxing, uplifting)
- Frankincense oil (relaxing, calming, uplifting, relieving anxiety)
- Geranium oil (uplifting, relaxing, sleep-inducing, energizing)
- Jasmine oil (antidepressant, calming, stress-relieving, uplifting)
- Lavender oil (uplifting, calming, relieving tension)
- Neroli oil (antidepressant, sleep-inducing, calming)
- Rose oil (uplifting, antidepressant, energizing)
- Valerian oil (calming, sleep-inducing)
- Ylang-ylang oil (relaxing, stress-relieving, uplifting)

VI. The Best and the Worst Careers for Highly Sensitive People and Empaths

In this section, you will find out which careers are the best for highly sensitive people and empaths, and which jobs should be avoided.

It is not so easy for all highly sensitive people and empaths to choose a career that they will love. Moreover, it is quite difficult for them to find a working place where they could feel safe and sound. This way, they will be able to perform well any tasks.

If you have to work in an office, you should choose your future work place very carefully considering all the traits of your sensitive personality and knowing that you will perceive the emotions of your coworkers and your boss. Some empaths can adapt themselves to the office work, while others may feel exhausted from communicating with a lot of people. And this factor may have an adverse effect on their physical and mental health.

The best careers for all highly sensitive people are low-stress, quiet working places (e.g. small companies with fewer people, or remote work) where all empaths will feel more comfortable. This way, they will be able to concentrate totally on their work. Being creative by nature, a lot of empaths can become good editors, writers, artists, or musicians. They can work as virtual assistants or accountants.

Some empaths prefer working as social workers, or nurses. On the one hand, such noble careers make them happy; on the other hand, they may feel exhausted since such jobs drain a lot of their energy.

- Interior designer
- Musician
- Photographer

Financial careers:
- Accountant
- Financial analyst
- Market researcher

Health-related careers:
- Dietician
- Druggist
- Massage therapist
- Naturopath
- Speech therapist

Nature-related careers:
- Botanist
- Biologist
- Ecologist

Trades:
- Carpenter
- Electrician
- Farmer
- Gardener
- Plumber

Technology careers:
- Graphic designer
- Programmer
- Social media manager

Writing-related careers:
- Blogger
- Editor
- Proofreader
- Writer (technical writer)

Other careers:
- Antiques appraiser
- Career coach
- Charity worker
- Clergyman
- Guidance counselor
- Life coach
- Librarian

- Mailman
- Pastry chef
- Physical therapist
- Psychologist
- Researcher

The ideal careers for highly sensitive people and empaths

As it was mentioned above, there is a wide variety of jobs which highly sensitive people and empaths can perform well and feel more or less happy. But there are jobs which can be rightly called the best for all empaths, the jobs where they will feel 100% happy.

Here are some of the best careers for all highly sensitive people and empaths:

1. Nurse

The innate trait of all highly sensitive people and empaths is to help others. They really enjoy it. Such people make good nurses. Since they know how to help their patients feel relaxed and can support them in word and deed. Highly sensitive people and empaths can work in a lot of places (such as hospitals, or nursing homes). They are able to support both patients and their family members in the moments of despair.

2. Psychologist

Another noble profession which is suitable for highly sensitive people is a psychologist. Such people help other overcome their fears and feel more confident. They help people to recover from mental illnesses which may have a negative effect on their physical health, if not treated in time. Since empaths are great listeners who feel all the depth of emotional suffering of other people, they will be able to support their patients and offer the right advice. Highly sensitive people and empaths can work in clinics, hospitals, or rehabilitation facilities or open their private practice.

3. Writer

If you love writing, and the power of words is important to you, you can share your emotions and feelings through writing articles, blogs, or books. Highly sensitive people generate ideas all the time drawing their inspiration from the universe. If empaths have the opportunity of expressing their creativity, they feel more energetic and happy. As a writer, you can write books or stories, work for a magazine and write articles, or even become a blogger.

4. Veterinarian

Empaths love nature and animals and tend to care for them. It is intolerable for them to see how animals suffer. If you have decided to work as a veterinarian, you will be able to heal sick animals in an animal hospital and give your moral support to their owners.

5. Artist

Artists can see the world in a different way compared to other people. Using the power of their vivid imagination, they will be able to create beautiful pictures that everyone will admire. Empaths make great artists since they are able to depict their profound vision of this world in a unique way creating their masterpieces. Empaths can work as book artists drawing their pictures for children books which kids will definitely love since everyone is attracted by their positive energy which is manifested in their artwork.

6. Musician (Composer)

Since all empaths adore music, it is natural that many of them become musicians and composers. All musicians are naturally creative and emotional people like writers and artists. They perceive music with all their heart. They can compose wonderful songs inspired by various people and events. Empaths communicate with their audience using the language of music. They may play the piano at a local restaurant, or concert hall to charge the grateful audience with their creative energy.

7. Life coach

Feeling deeply other people's emotions and needs, empaths can become perfect life coaches. They meet with people to help them make the right choice in life and to help them overcome fears and indecision on the way to fulfilling their dreams. Life coaches can work for a company or in a private way.

8. Guidance counselor

One of the best careers for highly sensitive people is a guidance counselor. They will be able to give children advice about their future careers that will change their lives. Empaths know what careers will suit the needs of other people, thus helping them make the right career choice. Empaths can work as guidance counselors at universities or local schools.

9. Teacher

Teacher is a noble profession since teachers share their valuable knowledge with their schoolchildren and inoculate them with moral principles which can be used in future. You can work as a teacher at a local school, or university.

Conclusion

In today's hectic world that is brimming with opportunities, everyone feels overloaded with information and exhausted from the never-ending pursuit of happiness and success. As a result, some people succeed in life, while others live in extreme poverty and suffer from poor physical and mental health. The more negative emotions they experience, the more miserable they feel. They may be kind-hearted, more talented than their successful friends and acquaintances, but they are too vulnerable. Sometimes such people may feel like aliens who don't belong to this planet. They feel detached from this world. They often suffer from loneliness, depression and anxiety, and these negative emotions and destructive thoughts block their way to happiness.

In this book you will learn about types of highly sensitive people, find out if you are one of them, and learn how to survive and thrive in this world being a highly sensitive person.

In the section 'Types of Highly Sensitive People', you will be able to find out what is the nature of highly sensitive people. You will also learn the difference between Empaths, Intuitives, Psychics (Clairvoyants, Clairaudients, and Mediums) and Spiritual Healers. You will also learn about the common traits of all types of highly sensitive people.

In the section 'Emotional Sensitivity Tests', you will find several tests that can be used to define whether you are a highly sensitive person, empath, intuitive, or spiritual healer. All you have to do is answer several questions included in the tests. You can take all of these tests, or choose only some of them. After realizing who you are in this world, you will start learning how to control your emotions so you can enjoy your life to the fullest.

In the section 'Survival Tips for Highly Sensitive People and Empaths', you will learn about the useful tips that will help all highly sensitive people and empaths cope with their sensitivity and control it to avoid physical and mental exhaustion that may cause serious diseases.

In the section 'The Eating Plan for Empaths and Highly Sensitive People', you will find out what foods can be eaten by highly sensitive people and empaths to improve your immune system, prevent serious diseases, decrease your sensitivity and increase your energy level. You will also find out what foods that have a detrimental effect on your physical and mental health should be excluded from your diet.

In the section 'Aromatherapy for Empaths and Highly Sensitive People', you will find out what essential oils can be used to boost your energy level, decrease your sensitivity, and neutralize the negative energy that you have accumulated from other people.

In the section 'The Best and the Worst Careers for Highly Sensitive People and Empaths', you will learn what careers to choose to be successful in life, and maintain good health.

By following these useful tips, you will be able to survive in this world and help other highly sensitive people to understand how important the role they play in this universe.

Thank you again for reading this book!

If you enjoyed this book I would really appreciate it if you would post a short review on Amazon.com. Your opinion is extremely important for me.

Copyright 2017 by Helena Snow - All rights reserved.

All rights Reserved. No part of this publication or the information in it may be quoted from or reproduced in any form by means such as printing, scanning, photocopying or otherwise without prior written permission of the copyright holder.

Disclaimer and Terms of Use: Effort has been made to ensure that the information in this book is accurate and complete, however, the author and the publisher do not warrant the accuracy of the information, text and graphics contained within the book due to the rapidly changing nature of science, research, known and unknown facts and internet. The Author and the publisher do not hold any responsibility for errors, omissions or contrary interpretation of the subject matter herein. This book is presented solely for motivational and informational purposes only.

79019116R00034

Made in the USA
San Bernardino, CA
10 June 2018